GRAMMAR
FOR
MINECRAFTERS

Activities to Help Kids Boost
Reading and Language Skills

Grades 1-2

ERIN FALLIGANT

Sky Pony Press
New York, New York

This book is not authorized or sponsored by Microsoft Corp., Mojang AB, Notch Development AB, or any other person or entity owning or controlling rights in the Minecraft name, trademark, or copyrights.

Copyright © 2023 by Hollan Publishing, Inc.

Minecraft® is a registered trademark of Notch Development AB.

The Minecraft game is copyright © Mojang AB.

All rights reserved. No part of this book may be reproduced in any manner without the express written consent of the publisher, except in the case of brief excerpts in critical reviews or articles. All inquiries should be addressed to Sky Pony Press, 307 West 36th Street, 11th Floor, New York, NY 10018.

Sky Pony Press books may be purchased in bulk at special discounts for sales promotion, corporate gifts, fund-raising, or educational purposes. Special editions can also be created to specifications. For details, contact the Special Sales Department, Sky Pony Press, 307 West 36th Street, 11th Floor, New York, NY 10018 or info@skyhorsepublishing.com.

Sky Pony® is a registered trademark of Skyhorse Publishing, Inc.®, a Delaware corporation.

Visit our website at www.skyponypress.com.

Authors, books, and more at SkyPonyPressBlog.com.

10 9 8 7 6 5 4 3 2 1

Library of Congress Cataloging-in-Publication Data is available on file.

Cover and interior illustration by Grace Sandford

Book design by Noora Cox

Print ISBN: 978-1-5107-7449-0

Printed in China

A NOTE TO PARENTS

Build their grammar skills, one fun activity at a time! When you want to reinforce classroom skills at home, it's crucial to have kid-friendly learning materials. This *Grammar for Minecrafters* workbook transforms grammar rules and language development into an irresistible adventure complete with diamond swords, zombies, skeletons, and ghasts. *Grammar for Minecrafters* is also fully aligned with National Common Core Standards for 1st and 2nd grade English Language Arts (ELA).

Encourage your child to progress at his or her own pace. Learning is best when students are challenged, but not frustrated. What's most important is that your Minecrafter is engaged in his or her own learning. With more than 50 gamer-friendly practice pages, puzzles, and familiar Minecraft characters on every page, your child will be eager to dive in and level up their reading, writing, and grammar skills.

Happy adventuring!

CONTENTS

NOUNS

A *noun* is a naming word. A noun names a person, place, animal, or thing.

Choose nouns from the box to fill in the blanks. Write the nouns.

hair	desert	~~girl~~	sword	llama

1. The _____ girl _____ held on tight.

2. The _____ ran so fast!

3. She held her _____ in the air.

4. Her _____

   blew in the wind.

5. Soon they would reach the

   _____.

PROPER NOUNS

The names of people, places, and pets are special. They are called *proper nouns.* Proper nouns start with capital letters.

Circle the proper noun in each sentence. Then draw a line under the first letter in that name.

1.  Steve has a fish.

2. This girl is Alex.

3. It is hot in the Nether.

4. Max is a dog.

5. Sam sees a spider.

SINGULAR AND PLURAL NOUNS

A *singular noun* names just one person, place, or thing. A *plural* noun names more than one person, place, or thing.

Circle five plural nouns in the story below. (*Hint:* Most plural nouns end with the letter *s*.]

The clock on the wall ticked. The spider blinked its red eyes. Class was almost over! There were three questions left on the test. The spider had two pencils. It wrote as many answers as it could. Good thing spiders have so many legs!

Write the plural nouns here:

eyes

MAKING PLURAL NOUNS

Add -s to most nouns to make them plural. Add -es to nouns that end in x, s, ch, or sh.

Circle the correct plural noun. Then write it on the line.

1. The rabbit finds the **carrots** .

   (carrots) carrotes

2. Many _____ stop at this bus stop.

   buss buses

3. A wither has three _____ .

   heads heades

4. A dolphin has zero _____ .

   legs leges

5. Alex hides in the _____ .

   bushs bushes

PRONOUNS

A *pronoun* is a word that takes the place of a noun.

Choose pronouns from the box to take the place of the underlined noun.

she	~~it~~	he	they	it

1. Alex and Steve build a <u>portal</u>. They hope

   it takes them to The End.

2. <u>Alex</u> jumps first because _____ is a very

   brave girl.

3. <u>Steve</u> is excited because _____ has

   never been there.

4. <u>Steve and Alex</u> know _____

   can find a way home.

5. Alex leaves her <u>axe</u> behind.

   She doesn't need _____ .

PLURAL PRONOUNS

Some pronouns take the place of more than one noun. They are called *plural pronouns.*

Read the sentence. Circle the plural pronoun that takes the place of the underlined word or words.

1. Steve and Alex are friends.

   (They)   Us   Them

2. She sees Endermen!

   they   them   him

3. Steve and I can juggle.

   we   I   He   Him   We

4. These snacks are for Alex and me.

   us   we   they

5. Spiders live in webs.

   It   Them   They

   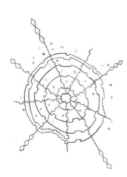

VERBS

A *verb* is an action word. A verb tells what a person, animal, or thing is doing.

Read each sentence, and circle the verb. Then write the verb.

1. Steve (jumps.)

   jumps

2. The pufferfish swims.

3. The dragon flies.

4. The zombie falls.

5. Alex drinks potion.

PRESENT TENSE VERBS

Verb tenses tell when actions happen. A *present tense verb* tells what is happening right now.

Read each sentence. Fill in the circle next to the present tense verb.

1. **The golem makes a snowball.**
   - ○ the
   - ● makes
   - ○ snowball

2. **The golem throws the ball.**
   - ○ golem
   - ○ ball
   - ○ throws

3. **The ball moves fast.**
   - ○ ball
   - ○ moves
   - ○ fast

4. **The zombie runs away.**
   - ○ runs
   - ○ zombie
   - ○ away

5. **The angry golem yells.**
   - ○ angry
   - ○ golem
   - ○ yells

PAST TENSE VERBS

A *past tense verb* tells what has already happened. Many verbs add -*ed* to show the past tense.

Example: Present-tense verb: crawl
Past-tense verb: crawled

Add -*ed* to write the past tense of each verb.

1. leap **ed**

2. paint

3. lick

4. walk

5. spawn

LINKING VERBS

Some verbs, like *linking verbs,* do not show action. They show what someone or something is like or how someone feels.

Choose linking verbs from the box to fill in the blanks. Write the linking verbs.

am	~~is~~	are	was	were

1. Redstone _is_ fun.

2. I _____ learning how to use it right now.

3. Yesterday zombies _____ close to my house.

4. I _____ afraid they would enter my house.

5. I used redstone and TNT

   to scare them away.

   Now there _____

   no more zombies!

SINGULAR AND PLURAL VERBS

A *singular verb* tells what one person, animal, or thing does. A *plural verb* tells what more than one person, animal, or thing does.

Look at each picture. Circle the correct verb to finish each sentence. Write it on the line.

1. Alex **rides** fast.

   ride (rides)

2. Chicken jockeys _____ chickens.

   ride   rides

3. The mob _____ a basket.

   shoot   shoots

4. Ghasts _____ fireballs.

   shoot   shoots

5. Witches _____ potions.

   brew   brews

6. This boy _____ potions, too.

   brew   brews

WRITE THE RIGHT VERB

Each sentence has a singular or plural verb. Fix the verb and write it on the line.

1. Blazes *spawns* in the Nether.

spawn

2. Steve *aim* his bow at a blaze.

3. The blaze *float* in the air.

4. The blaze *shoot* fireballs.

5. Steve's arrows *hits* the blaze.

6. Steve *save* the day!

ADJECTIVE

An *adjective* is a describing word. An adjective describes a person, place, or thing.

Choose adjectives from the box to fill in the blanks. Write the adjectives.

heavy	wavy	long	~~red~~	square

1. Steve's house has a red roof.

2. It has _____ windows.

3. Steve walks down the _____ sidewalk.

4. He carries a _____ pickaxe.

5. Steve has _____ hair.

USE YOUR SENSES

Adjectives can describe how something looks, sounds, tastes, smells, or feels.

Choose an adjective to finish each sentence. Circle the adjective.

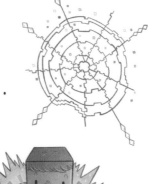

1. The ice cream tastes _sweet_ .

   (sweet)　salty

2. The cobweb feels _____ .

   tall　　sticky

3. The gold looks _____ .

   blue　　shiny

4. The dragon's roar sounds _____ .

   loud　　old

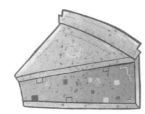

5. The pie smells _____ .

   sweet　　big

ADJECTIVES THAT COMPARE

Some adjectives tell how nouns are different. You can add *-er* to many adjectives to compare two nouns.

Example: small and smaller

Add *-er* to compare these nouns. Write the new adjective.

1. The dragon is smart. Alex is

   smarter .

2. The shulker is fast. Alex is

   _____ .

3. The dog is soft. The cat is

   _____ .

4. The boy is tall. The tree is

   _____ .

5. An iron axe is strong. A diamond axe is

   _____ .

COMPARING MORE THAN TWO

You can add *-est* to many adjectives to compare *more* than two nouns.

Example: small, smaller, smallest

Circle all the comparative adjectives with -er or -est.

Steve is tired and wants a bed. One bed looks soft. The next bed looks (softer) The last bed looks softest. He sits down on the beds. One bed feels strong. The next bed feels stronger. The last bed feels strongest. He lays down on the beds. One bed is long. The next bed is longer. The last bed is longest. He climbs into the last bed and goes to sleep.

POSSESSIVE NOUNS

A *possessive noun* shows that something belongs to a person, animal, or thing. To make most possessive nouns, add an apostrophe (') and the letter *s*.

Example: The axe belongs to Steve. It is Steve's axe.

Circle the possessive noun in the sentence. Then write the possessive noun.

1. Alex's dog likes treats.

Alex's

2. The villager's emerald is shiny.

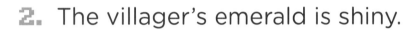

3. The guardian's spikes are sharp.

4. The wolf's fur is thick.

5. The zombie's skin is green.

PLURAL POSSESSIVE NOUNS

A *plural possessive noun* shows that something belongs to more than one person, animal, or thing. To make most plural possessive nouns, add an apostrophe (') after the s.

Example: The well belongs to the villagers. It is the villagers' well.

Circle all the plural possessive nouns.
Hint: **They end in an apostrophe (').**

How can you tell a zombie villager from a villager? Look and listen. Zombie villagers' robes are tattered. Villagers' robe are not. Zombie villagers' skin is green. Villagers' skin is not. Zombie villagers' groans are loud. Villagers don't groan at all. See the difference?

How many plural possessives did you circle?

23

ARTICLES

A, an, and *the* are words that come before nouns. They are called *articles.* Write *a* before nouns that name one person, place, or thing. Write *the* before nouns that name more than one.

Example: a bucket of fish   the buckets of fish

Circle *a* before a word that names one. Circle *the* before a word that names more than one.

1. We saw **the** dolphins.

    a   (the)

2. We fed one _____ piece of fish.

    a   the

3. It led us to _____ chest.

    a   the

4. We saw _____ emeralds inside.

    a   the

5. It was _____ treasure chest!

    a   the

A OR AN?

Write *an* before nouns that begin with *a, e, i, o,* or *u.*

Example: a mushroom   an ice cream cone

Which is correct? Circle the correct article.

1. We picked _____*an*_____ apple from the tree.

   a   (an)

2. We grew _____ carrot in the garden.

   a   an

3. We found _____ egg in the chicken coop.

   a   an

4. I used _____ spoon to eat my stew.

   a   an

5. We shared _____ cookie for dessert.

   a   an

PREPOSITIONS

A *preposition* is a word that tells *where* someone or something is.

Choose a preposition from the box to finish each sentence. Write the preposition.

~~on~~	onto	under	up	beside

1. The cat crouched **on** the lily pad.

2. He stood _____ the zombie.

3. Alex climbed _____ the wall.

4. Steve looked _____ at the ghast.

5. He slept _____ the covers.

MINE FOR PREPOSITIONS

Circle all the words that tell *where* someone or something is. Can you find 8 prepositions?

 under

 Steve

 below

 on

 in

 over

 fast

 behind

 dragon

 mob

 near

 inside

SENTENCES

A sentence is a group of words that tells a complete idea. A sentence starts with a capital letter.

Example: ✔ Alex had a cat. (sentence)
✘ a cat Alex (not a sentence)

Circle *yes* if the words make a sentence. Circle *no* if they do not make a sentence.

1. a wild cat

yes   (no)

2. You can tame a wolf.

yes   no

3. Wolves eat bones.

yes   no

4. the tasty fish

yes   no

5. Dogs wear collars.

yes   no

6. bones and fish

yes   no

7. Pets are fun.

yes   no

WORD ORDER

Read each group of words. Which sentence makes sense? Fill in the circle next to the sentence.

1. ○ here. will bus The stop
   ● The bus will stop here.
   ○ The stop will bus here.

2. ○ The slime will wait.
   ○ slime wait. will The
   ○ The wait. will slime

3. ○ The bus. slime the rides
   ○ slime bus. the rides The
   ○ The slime rides the bus.

4. ○ slime bag. has The a
   ○ The slime has a bag.
   ○ slime The bag. a has

5. ○ goes bus The to school.
   ○ The bus goes to school.
   ○ The school. goes to bus

ALL MIXED UP

These words are mixed up! Put them in order. Write each sentence below.

1. has   dog.   a   Steve

Steve has a dog.

2. lava   is   The   hot.

3. mad.   ghast   The   is

4. fast!   Alex   is

5. paint.   This   likes   mob   to

TELLING SENTENCES AND QUESTIONS

A telling sentence tells something. It ends with a period (.). A question is a sentence that asks something. It ends with a question mark (?).

Finish each sentence. Add a period if it is a telling sentence. Add a question mark if it is a question.

1. Alex found a chest .

2. Was it full of treasure

3. Alex brought it home

4. She looked inside

5. What did she see

COMMANDS

A *command* is a sentence that tells or asks someone to do something.

Examples: Go to bed.
Will you make your bed?

Match the words on the left with the words on the right. Draw a line to complete each command.

1. Build a   a. emeralds?

2. Light it with   b. mobs.

3. Don't go out at   c. house.

4. Look out for   d. torches.

5. Will you mine for   e. night.

EXCLAMATIONS

An *exclamation* is a sentence that that shows strong feelings such as surprise or fear. It ends with an exclamation mark (!).

Examples: Watch out!
Run away from that mob!

Look at each picture. Finish the sentence with a word and an exclamation mark.

1. Look! That wither is reading

    three _**books!**_

2. No way! That Enderman knows

    how to _____

3. Ouch! That lava is so

    _____

4. Wow! Steve caught a really big

    _____

5. Look out! A zombie just spawned

    from that _____

COMPOUND SENTENCES

A *compound sentence* joins two smaller sentences.

Underline the two smaller sentences in each compound sentence.

1. <u>The shulker chases Alex</u>, but <u>she is too fast</u>.

2. The golem will dribble the ball, or he will shoot it.

3. Some mushrooms are brown, and some mushrooms are red.

4. The lava is hot, but Steve can jump over it.

5. Alex is hurt, so she drinks a potion of healing.

CONJUNCTIONS

Conjunctions are joining words. They join the two sentences in a compound sentence.

Choose a conjunction from the box to join the parts of the sentence. Write it on the line.

or	~~and~~	but	so

1. She looked out the window, **and**

   she saw something.

2. It was dark, _____ she knew

   something was outside.

3. Was it a mob, _____ was it

   a critter?

4. She saw four eyes, _____

   she knew there were two

   mobs. Endermen!

CAPITAL LETTERS

The first word of a sentence begins with a capital letter. The names of people, places, and pets begin with capital letters, too.

Read each sentence. Which word needs a capital letter? Fill in the circle next to that word.

1. This cat likes alex.
   - ○ Cat
   - ○ Likes
   - ● Alex

2. she likes cats, too.
   - ○ She
   - ○ Likes
   - ○ Cats

3. Her cat is leo.
   - ○ Cat
   - ○ Is
   - ○ Leo

4. i want to play with Leo.
   - ○ I
   - ○ Want
   - ○ Play

5. They walk to Silverfish park.
   - ○ To
   - ○ Walk
   - ○ Park

THE WORD I

The word I is always capitalized. Write a capital I even if the word is in the middle of a sentence.

Example: At school, I saw my friends.

Look at the pictures. Finish each sentence with a capital I and something you might see.

1. In the swamp, __I__ saw

   a __witch__ .

2. On a lily pad, _____ saw

   a _____ .

3. In the forest, _____ saw

   a _____ .

4. At school, my friends and _____

   saw a _____ .

5. By the igloo, _____ saw a

   _____ .

PEOPLE AND TITLES

A person's first and last name begin with a capital letter. Titles begin with capital letters, too.

Examples: Jack Smith
                   Ms. Parker
                   Dr. Jones
                   Uncle John

Circle every name or title that needs to be capitalized.

(ethan) enderman was having a bad night. He was moving blocks around with his friends. He hurt his back. mrs. enderman called dr. wither, but dr. wither was busy. He was taking care of aunt edna. dr. blaze came to visit instead, but dr. blaze went to the wrong house! molly magma helped the endermans. She showed dr. blaze where ethan enderman lived.

PLACES

The names of cities and states begin with a capital letter. The names of streets begin with a capital letter, too.

Examples: Samuel Slime
13 Swamp Street
Madison, Wisconsin 12345

Find mistakes in the addresses below. Circle the letters that should be capitals.

1. Harold Husk
456 Cactus Lane
Phoenix, Arizona 54321

2. Wyatt Wolf
123 Igloo Drive
Anchorage, alaska 11111

3. Paul Piglin
566 nether Circle
Honolulu, Hawaii 55555

4. Skylar Squid
111 Squirt Street
Miami, florida 12345

5. Steve Smith
654 Pickaxe parkway
Boise, Idaho 54433

DATES

Days, months, and dates begin with a capital letter. Holidays begin with a capital letter, too.

Examples: Monday
January 2
Wednesday, February 14
Valentine's Day

Answer each question with a day, month, or date. Don't forget the capital letter!

1. What is your favorite day of the week?

Saturday

2. When is your birthday?

3. What is the date today?

4. What day of the week is it today?

5. What is your favorite holiday?

BOOK AND MOVIE TITLES

All important words in book and movie titles begin with a capital letter. The first and last words of a title are always capitalized.

Examples: *Steve Goes to the Nether*
Learn to Build a Treehouse

Circle each letter that needs to be capitalized.

1. (a)ttack of the (e)ndermen

2. how to rob a mob

3. goodnight griefer

4. mine your business

5. one fish, two fish, red fish, pufferfish

Come up with your own funny book title. Write it here.

_____

_____

_____

COMMAS IN A LIST

Use a comma (,) between words in a list. Write the comma before the word *and.*

Example: I ate a carrot, an apple, and a cookie for lunch.

Each sentence is missing commas. Write a comma between each word in a list.

1. I raised horses, chickens, and pigs.

2. I grew potatoes carrots pumpkins and watermelons.

3. I visited the desert the jungle and the swamp.

4. I ran into witches slimes and zombies.

5. Good thing I brought my potions my shield and my sword.

COMMAS IN DATES AND LETTERS

Use a comma between the day and the year. Use a comma after the greeting and the closing of a letter.

Example: November 7, 1969
                         Dear Alex,
                         From, Steve

Write commas where they belong in the letter.

June 29, 2022

Dear Steve

I am having a great time at the beach. I went boating swimming

and sailing. A dolphin led us to buried treasure! We found

emeralds diamonds and gold. Maybe I will share some with you.

Your friend

Alex

COLLECTIVE NOUNS

A *collective noun* names a group of people, animals, or things.

Choose a word from the box to fill in each blank. Write the collective noun.

row	batch	team	pile	~~school~~

1. Steve swam past a _school_ of fish.

2. The basketball _____ won the game.

3. Your health bar shows a _____ of hearts.

4. She made a _____ of pies for the bake sale.

5. A _____ of eggs lay on the ground.

PEOPLE, ANIMALS, OR THINGS?

**Read the story below. Circle the *collective nouns*
(all the words that name a group of people, animals,
or things).**

The farmer went to the village to trade. There was a
crowd of villagers in the market. He traded a bunch
of carrots. He traded a pile of potatoes. What did
he get? He got a stack of emeralds. He bought wool
from the shepherd's flock of sheep. He bought
beef from the butcher's herd of cows. He bought a
batch of bread. It was enough to feed a whole family
of villagers!

IRREGULAR PLURAL NOUNS

An *irregular plural noun* has special spelling.

Draw a line to match each noun with its irregular plural noun.

1. loaf

2. child

3. foot

4. woman

5. wolf

6. mouse

7. goose

8. man

9. cactus

a. geese

b. mice

c. cacti

d. men

e. children

f. women

g. loaves

h. feet

i. wolves

ONE SHEEP, TWO SHEEP

Some plural nouns are spelled the same as the singular nouns. The other words in the sentence tell you if the noun names one thing or more than one.

Examples: *sheep, fish,* and *deer*

Read the sentence. Circle "singular" if the underlined noun names one. Circle "plural" if the noun names more than one.

1. A <u>deer</u> slept in the grass.

    plural

2. You can dye the wool from <u>sheep</u>.

   singular   plural

3. Steve caught a <u>fish</u>.

   singular   plural

4. Alex had a pink <u>sheep</u>.

   singular   plural

5. Tropical <u>fish</u> live in the ocean.

   singular   plural

6. You might see lots of <u>deer</u> in the forest.

   singular   plural

REFLEXIVE PRONOUNS

A *reflexive pronoun* shows when people, animals, or mobs do something to or for themselves.

Example: A zombie fell in a trap and hurt *himself.*

Choose a word from the box to fill in each blank. Write the reflexive pronoun.

| herself | itself | ~~myself~~ | ourselves | themselves |

1. I made mushroom stew for

   myself .

2. Alex and Steve were proud of

   _____ .

3. A dog can't give _____ a treat.

4. Steve and I are building a treehouse

   by _____ .

5. Alex crafted a sword for _____ .

WRITE THE RIGHT PRONOUN

Each sentence below has the wrong reflexive pronoun. Can you fix it?

Write the correct pronoun. *Hint:* **Use a word from the box on p. 48.**

1. The girl used a potion to protect <u>myself</u>.

   herself

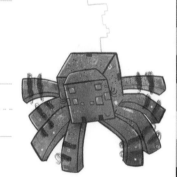

2. I ate the whole batch of cookies <u>himself</u>.

3. The spider made <u>themselves</u> a web.

4. We dressed <u>myself</u> in armor.

5. Steve and his friends kept the treasure for <u>ourselves</u>.

PAST TENSE IRREGULAR VERBS

A *past tense irregular verb* tells about something that already happened, but it does *not* end in *-ed*. It has a special spelling.

Example: fly (present tense)
flew (past tense)

Draw a line to match each verb with its irregular past tense verb.

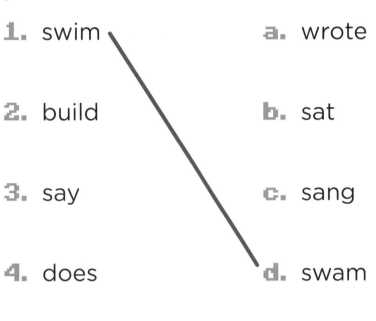

1. swim
2. build
3. say
4. does
5. write
6. sing
7. go
8. sit

a. wrote
b. sat
c. sang
d. swam
e. did
f. said
g. built
h. went

CHOOSE THE RIGHT VERB

Read each sentence. Circle the correct past tense verb to finish the sentence. Write it on the line.

1. He wanted to hide behind the tree, but

   we _hid_ there yesterday.

   (hid)   hided

2. Can I ride the chicken? No, you already

   _____ it once.

   rided   rode

3. Ghasts can fly! One _____

   past me this morning.

   flyed   flew

4. This boy can't sleep! But he

   _____ well last night.

   slept   sleeped

5. The snow golem throws the last snowball.

   It already _____ five snowballs.

   throwed   threw

ADVERBS

An *adverb* describes an action. An adverb tells how, where, and when an action happens. Many adverbs end in *-ly.*

Read this story. Circle the adverbs. (*Hint*: They end in *-ly.*)

Alex stepped (slowly) toward the shulker. She waited patiently for its shell to open. Suddenly, the shulker opened its shell. Alex quickly raised her sword. The shulker growled angrily. It shot green bullets. Alex dropped her sword. She ran away swiftly!

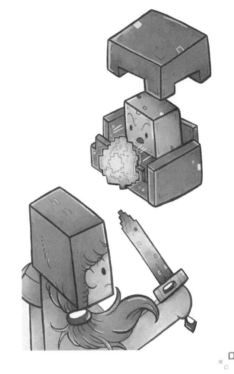

How many adverbs did you circle?

ADVERB OR ADJECTIVE?

An *adverb* is different from an adjective. An *adjective* describes a person, place, or thing. An *adverb* describes an action.

Read each sentence. Is the underlined word an adjective or an adverb? Circle the correct answer.

1. The <u>orange</u> cat sat by Alex.

   (adjective)   adverb

2. The cat sat <u>patiently</u>.

   adjective   adverb

3. The pufferfish swam <u>quickly</u>.

   adjective   adverb

4. The <u>round</u> pufferfish swam.

   adjective   adverb

5. The <u>hot</u> blaze flew toward Steve.

   adjective   adverb

6. Steve fought <u>bravely</u>.

   adjective   adverb

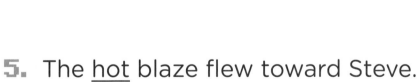

QUOTATION MARKS

Quotation marks (" ") show the exact words someone says. They go before the first word and after the last word spoken.

Read each sentence. Underline the words the speaker says. Add quotation marks before and after those words.

1. **"**<u>Hey, Steve! Come see what I found!</u>**"** said Alex.

2. What is it? asked Steve.

3. Emeralds! said Alex.

4. Where did you find them? asked Steve.

5. It's a secret, said Alex with a smile.

IF MOBS COULD TALK

Imagine that mobs could talk. What would they say?

Draw a line to match the mob with the words it might say. Put quotation marks around the words.

1. Witch

2. Zombie villager

3. Guardian

4. Iron golem

5. Enderman

a. Try to catch me. I can teleport!

b. I am made of a carved pumpkin and iron blocks.

c. "I brewed something just for you."

d. I feel strange. Does anyone have a golden apple?

e. Stay away from my ocean monument. I have my eye on you!

POEMS AND SONG TITLES

Write quotation marks before and after the title of a poem or a song.

Example: "Old MacEnderman Had a Farm"

Read each sentence. Write quotation marks around the title of each poem or song.

1. They sang "Baa, Baa, Pink Sheep" all the way to the farm.

2. Steve wrote a poem called Blaze, Blaze, Go Away.

3. They sang The Itsy Bitsy Cave Spider as they crept through the cave.

4. When he couldn't sleep, he said the words to Twinkle, Twinkle Little Stone.

5. Alex hummed The Zombie Went Over the Mountain while she waited.

COLONS

When you write the time, use a colon (:) between the hour and the minutes.

Example: 9:00 in the morning

Read each sentence. Write the time in numerals on the line. Add a colon where it's needed.

1. Breakfast starts at seven o'clock in the morning.

7:00

2. Alex eats lunch at twelve fifteen.

3. Steve's juggling act starts at four thirty today.

4. Bedtime is at eight thirty sharp!

5. Mobs spawn at nine o'clock at night.

CONTRACTIONS

A *contraction* is two words made into one word. A letter or letters are taken out, and an apostrophe (') takes their place.

Example: Please do not feed the dog.
Please *don't* feed the dog.

Draw a line to match each contraction with the words it replaces.

1. can't
2. won't
3. he'd
4. you're
5. doesn't

a. he had
b. does not
c. can not
d. you are
e. will not

PICK A CONTRACTION

Choose a contraction from the box to fill in each blank. Write the contraction.

| Let's | ~~It's~~ | She's | We'll | He'd |

1. Try jumping in the portal.

   It's fun!

2. _____ like to eat Alex's chicken.

3. Our hunger bar is low. _____ eat something.

4. Alex keeps fighting. _____ not giving up.

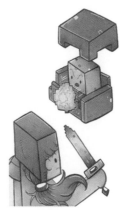

5. Our house is burning. _____ have to build another one.

ABBREVIATIONS OF STREET NAMES

You can shorten a street name with an *abbreviation.* Write a period (.) after the abbreviation.

Examples: Street = St.   Avenue = Ave.
                Road = Rd.   Lane = Ln.
                Drive = Dr.   Court = Ct.

Read each sentence. Write the abbreviation for the underlined street name.

1. Alex left his house on

    Cobblestone <u>Court</u>.   **Ct.**

2. He went fishing at a pond on

    Salmon <u>Street</u>.

3. He tamed a wolf along Forest <u>Drive</u>.

4. He dodged a witch's potion on Swamp <u>Road</u>.

5. He mined for blocks below Emerald <u>Avenue</u>.

6. He put out a fire on Lava <u>Lane</u>.

ABBREVIATIONS OF TITLES

You can shorten a person's title with an abbreviation. Write a period (.) after the abbreviation.

Examples: Dr., Mr., Mrs., Ms.

Note: **Do not write a period after the title "Miss" unless it's at the end of a sentence.**

Read each sentence. Circle the title before each person's name. Write a period after the titles that need periods.

1. (Mr.) Brown trades goods for emeralds.

2. Dr McIntire cured the zombie villager.

3. Ms Strict passed out the tests.

4. Mrs Farmer baked a pumpkin pie.

5. Miss Alex rode to the rescue!

ANSWER KEY

PAGE 6
1. girl
2. llama
3. sword
4. hair
5. desert

PAGE 7
1. <u>S</u>teve
2. <u>A</u>lex
3. <u>N</u>ether
4. <u>M</u>ax
5. <u>S</u>am

PAGE 8
Eyes, questions, pencils, answers, spiders, legs

PAGE 9
1. carrots
2. buses
3. heads
4. legs
5. bushes

PAGE 10
1. it
2. she
3. he
4. they
5. it

PAGE 11
1. They
2. them
3. We
4. us
5. They

PAGE 12
1. jumps
2. swims
3. flies
4. falls
5. drinks

PAGE 13
1. makes
2. throws
3. moves
4. runs
5. yells

PAGE 14
1. leaped
2. painted
3. licked
4. walked
5. spawned

PAGE 15
1. is
2. am
3. were
4. was
5. are

PAGE 16
1. rides
2. ride
3. shoots
4. shoot
5. brew
6. brews

PAGE 17
1. spawn
2. aims
3. floats
4. shoots
5. hit
6. saves

PAGE 18
1. red
2. square
3. long
4. heavy
5. wavy

PAGE 19
1. sweet
2. sticky
3. shiny
4. loud
5. sweet

PAGE 20
1. smarter
2. faster
3. softer
4. taller
5. stronger

PAGE 21
soft, softer, softest, strong, stronger, strongest, long, longer, longest

PAGE 22
1. Alex's
2. villager's
3. guardian's
4. wolf's
5. zombie's

PAGE 23
1. villagers'
2. villagers'
3. villagers'
4. villagers'
5. villagers'

PAGE 24
1. the
2. a
3. a
4. the
5. a

PAGE 25
1. an
2. a
3. an
4. a
5. a

PAGE 26
1. on
2. beside
3. onto
4. up
5. under

PAGE 27
under, below, on, over, in,
behind, near, inside

PAGE 28
1. no
2. yes
3. yes
4. no
5. yes
6. no
7. yes

PAGE 29
1. The bus will stop here.
2. The slime will wait.
3. The slime rides the bus.
4. The slime has a bag.
5. The bus goes to school.

PAGE 30
1. Steve has a dog.
2. The lava is hot.
3. The ghast is mad.
4. Alex is fast!
5. This mob likes to paint.

PAGE 31
1. .
2. ?
3. .
4. .
5. ?

PAGE 32
1. c
2. d
3. e
4. b
5. a

PAGE 33
1. books!
2. paint!
3. hot!
4. fish!
5. egg!

PAGE 34
1. <u>The shulker chases Alex</u>, but <u>she is too fast.</u>
2. <u>The golem will dribble the ball</u>, or <u>he will shoot it.</u>
3. <u>Some mushrooms are brown</u>, and <u>some mushrooms are red.</u>
4. <u>The lava is hot</u>, but <u>Steve can jump over it.</u>
5. <u>Alex is hurt</u>, so <u>she drinks a potion of healing.</u>

PAGE 35
1. and
2. but
3. or
4. so

PAGE 36
1. Alex
2. She
3. Leo
4. I
5. Park

PAGE 37
Note: Answers may vary.
1. I, witch
2. I, cat
3. I, tree
4. I, spider
5. I, polar bear

PAGE 38
1. Ethan Enderman
2. Mrs. Enderman
3. Dr. Wither
4. Dr. Wither
5. Aunt Edna
6. Dr. Blaze
7. Dr. Blaze
8. Molly Magma
9. Endermans
10. Dr. Blaze
11. Ethan Enderman

PAGE 39
1. Cactus Lane
2. Alaska
3. Nether
4. Florida
5. Parkway

PAGE 40
Answers may vary.

PAGE 41
1. Attack of the Endermen
2. How to Rob a Mob
3. Goodnight Griefer
4. Mine Your Business
5. One Fish, Two Fish, Red Fish, Pufferfish

PAGE 42
1. I raised horses, chickens, and pigs.
2. I grew potatoes, carrots, pumpkins, and watermelons.
3. I visited the desert, the jungle, and the swamp.
4. I ran into witches, slimes, and zombies.
5. Good thing I brought my potions, my shield, and my sword.

PAGE 43
June 29, 2022
Dear Steve,
I am having a great time at the beach. I went boating, swimming, and sailing. A dolphin led us to buried treasure! We found emeralds, diamonds, and gold. Maybe I will share some with you.
Your friend,
Alex

PAGE 44
1. school
2. team
3. row
4. batch
5. pile

PAGE 45
crowd, bunch, pile, stack, flock, herd, batch, family

PAGE 46
1. g
2. e
3. h
4. f
5. i
6. b
7. a
8. d
9. c

PAGE 47
1. singular
2. plural
3. singular
4. singular
5. plural
6. plural

PAGE 48
1. myself
2. themselves
3. itself
4. ourselves
5. herself

PAGE 49
1. herself
2. myself
3. itself
4. ourselves
5. themselves

PAGE 50
1. d
2. g
3. f
4. e
5. a
6. c
7. h
8. b

PAGE 51
1. hid
2. rode
3. flew
4. slept
5. threw

PAGE 52
slowly, patiently, suddenly, quickly, angrily, swiftly (6 adverbs)

PAGE 53
1. adjective
2. adverb
3. adverb
4. adjective
5. adjective
6. adverb

PAGE 54
1. "Hey, Steve! Come see what I found!" said Alex.
2. "What is it?" asked Steve.
3. "Emeralds!" said Alex.
4. "Where did you find them?" asked Steve.
5. "It's a secret," said Alex with a smile.

PAGE 55
1. c. "I brewed something just for you."
2. d. "I feel strange. Does anyone have a golden apple?"
3. e. "Stay away from my ocean monument. I have my eye on you!"
4. b. "I am made of a carved pumpkin and iron blocks."
5. a. "Try to catch me. I can teleport!"

PAGE 56
1. "Baa, Baa, Pink Sheep"
2. "Blaze, Blaze, Go Away"
3. "The Itsy Bitsy Cave Spider"
4. "Twinkle, Twinkle Little Stone"
5. "The Zombie Went Over the Mountain"

PAGE 57
1. 7:00
2. 12:15
3. 4:30
4. 8:30
5. 9:00

PAGE 58
1. c
2. e
3. a
4. d
5. b

PAGE 59
1. It's
2. He'd
3. Let's
4. She's
5. We'll

PAGE 60
1. Ct.
2. St.
3. Dr.
4. Rd.
5. Ave.
6. Ln.

PAGE 61
1. Mr.
2. Dr.
3. Ms.
4. Mrs.
5. Miss